ART REVOLUTIONS
POP ART

Linda Bolton

PETER BEDRICK BOOKS
NTC/Contemporary Publishing Group
NEW YORK

This American edition published 2000 by Peter Bedrick Books,
a division of NTC/Contemporary Publishing Group, Inc.,
4255 West Touhy Avenue, Lincolnwood (Chicago),
Illinois 60646-1975 U.S.A.

First published in Great Britain in 2000 by Belitha Press Limited,
London House, Great Eastern Wharf, Parkgate Road, London SW11 4NQ

Editor Susie Brooks
Designer Helen James
Picture Researcher Diana Morris
Educational Consultant Hester Collicutt
Consultants for US Edition Nathaniel Harris, Ruth Nason

Printed in China

International Standard Book Number: 0-87226-614-1

Library of Congress Cataloging-in-Publication data
is available from the United States Library of Congress.

00 01 02 03   15 14 13 12 11 10 9 8 7 6 5 4 3 2 1

Picture Credits:

CONTENTS

Pop Explosion!   4

Roy Lichtenstein   8

Andy Warhol   10

Claes Oldenburg   12

Allan D'Arcangelo   14

Tom Wesselmann   16

James Rosenquist   18

Richard Hamilton   20

Peter Blake   22

Patrick Caulfield   24

David Hockney   26

More Pop   28

Find Out More   30

Index   32

Useful words are explained on page 30.

POP EXPLOSION!

Pop Art dominated the 1960s. It was created by artists who enjoyed the type of images seen in advertisements, movies, and other modern forms of communication. Pop artists made pictures and objects that were as bright and bold as comic strips or soup cans, celebrating the modern way of life.

By the late 1950s, the United States and Britain had recovered from World War II and become prosperous societies. Technology made it possible for factories to mass-produce goods that millions of ordinary people could afford. Bright, bold designs and pictures were everywhere – on packaging and ads, in movies and magazines, and on posters and TV.

Most established artists ignored this popular trend. In the 1950s, American artists were the leading figures of Abstract Expressionism, a type of painting which expressed private emotions. Then, in the late 1950s and the 1960s, the Pop artists burst in on the scene in the United States and Britain, producing colorful images of things like cars, hamburgers, and movie stars.

CLAES OLDENBURG

Leaning Fork with Meatball and Spaghetti I

1994, painted aluminum

Pop Art was at its height in the 1960s, but some Pop artists continued to work in the style. Claes Oldenburg made this giant fork and meatball in 1994. It is around six feet high – more than ten times lifesize – and is made of metal. Besides sculptures of food, Oldenburg also made "soft sculptures" of normally hard objects, such as typewriters. The sculptures make us see ordinary objects in new ways.

Pop Art was not about private emotions, though it did make people feel that modern living was fun. At first, critics disliked Pop, and attacked the artists for taking over mass-produced images that were not made by them. But the energy and cheerfulness of Pop Art appealed to ordinary people. Pop became accepted, and some Pop artists were treated like stars.

ROY LICHTENSTEIN

Whaam!

1963, acrylic paint on canvas

Many Pop artists experimented with new techniques and materials. Roy Lichtenstein used modern acrylic paints to make huge, striking pictures that look like blown-up sections from comic strips. This canvas is more than twelve feet wide. The colors are simple, flat, and eye-catching. Everything is outlined in black, so the images stand out clearly. Some areas are painted in dots. Lichtenstein did this to make his pictures look like machine-made color prints.

Pop used everyday images that people were familiar with from movies, ads, and other such sources. But most Pop artists made subtle changes to the images, or combined them, to get new effects. Some of the artists painted in oils, but many preferred working with modern materials such as vinyl, acrylics, or aluminum.

They favored techniques such as collage – pictures made by cutting out photos and similar images and pasting them together to make a new composition. And they liked prints, used to produce the same picture many times.

ANDY WARHOL

Four Colored Campbell's Soup Can

1965, silkscreen print on canvas

Convenience foods (almost ready to eat) were already very popular in the 1960s. Andy Warhol was a big fan of Campbell's soup. He made many silkscreen prints of Campbell's distinctive cans, showing the familiar brand name and logo. Here he has copied a bold image advertising a can of tomato soup. It is big and striking – around three feet tall. Warhol has changed the label by using different colors. He has also handpainted some areas, so the lines are slightly wobbly. This shows us that we are not looking at a mass-produced poster. Warhol has created an original work of art.

ROBERT INDIANA

The American Dream I

1961, oil paint on canvas

This is one of a series of pictures that Robert Indiana painted as a tribute to the United States. Born Robert Clark, this artist even took on the name of his home state! This painting is made up of words and symbols from American pinball machines. The big, colorful images suggest the lights flashing on and off in a pinball game. They make us think of the noise, glare, and lively music of a busy amusement arcade.

ANDY WARHOL

Marilyn Diptych (detail)

1962, silkscreen print on canvas

The Pop artists often made pictures of famous people, in the style of posters on billboards and teenage bedroom walls. Marilyn Monroe was one of the most famous movie stars of the 1950s. Warhol used a black and white photo, adding his own colors. In some Warhol works using this image, Marilyn's portrait is repeated 50 times, as if to suggest that she was a manufactured product, just like a soup can.

ROY LICHTENSTEIN (USA) 1923–1997

Roy Lichtenstein became fascinated by comics, from the adventures of Superman to stories about war and romance. Originally an art teacher and Abstract Expressionist painter, he started copying cartoon characters from comics and candy wrappers to amuse his sons. Then he blew up small comic pictures into big, wall-sized paintings, giving them the firm outlines and solid colors of comics. He even painted in the background dots created by crude printing processes. Out of cheap magazines, Lichtenstein created paintings that sold for large sums.

Mr. Bellamy

1961, oil paint on canvas

This picture looks like one frame from a comic-strip story. The words in the thought bubble tell us that the officer is wondering what someone called Mr. Bellamy is like – and Lichtenstein lets us wonder, also. We do not know who Mr. Bellamy is, or why the officer must report to him. The picture probably comes from a real comic book. By painting just one frame from the story, Lichtenstein lets us imagine what will happen next. The single image is like a flash of a scene you might catch when flicking between different television channels with a remote control.

AMERICAN COMICS

Comic strips are at least 200 years old. For a long time "the funnies" really were intended to make people laugh. But later on, stories of superheroes, war, and romance became just as popular – not comic at all, though we still use the word. The modern style of comic book became a firm favorite after Superman appeared in 1938.

Drowning Girl
1963, oil and acrylic paints on canvas

This is a scene from a romantic comic strip. The thought bubble shows us that the drowning girl would rather sink than call Brad for help. We do not know who Brad is, but we guess that the girl is in love with him and that he has done something to upset her. In spite of what she says, she really wants him to save her. Will Brad come to the rescue? We are not really left in suspense, because this kind of romantic story always has a happy ending. Lichtenstein has frozen the scene in striking close-up, emphasizing the feeling of disaster. He has used bold outlines and strong, simple colors to add to the dramatic effect.

This sunrise over water is another picture you might expect to see in a comic. Again the picture is simplified, broken down into the primary colors – red, yellow, and blue. Some areas, such as the sun's rays and the water, are solid color. Other areas, such as the sky, are made up of rows of regular dots. Lichtenstein created this image by lithography, a printmaking process often used in comics and posters.

Sunrise
1965, offset lithograph

9

ANDY WARHOL (USA) 1928–1987

"I want to be a machine."

Andy Warhol was one of the most famous Pop artists. His first job was as an illustrator, working for fashion magazines. In 1955 he had an exhibition of shoe pictures where each one was named after a celebrity.

Warhol loved the movies and even made movies himself. In his art, he used modern techniques, such as silkscreen printing, which enabled him to mass-produce images, like a machine. He called his studio "The Factory."

Triple Elvis

1962, silkscreen print on canvas

Elvis Presley was a pin-up in the late 1950s and 1960s. He was not only a great rock-and-roll singer, but also the star of many movies. Here Warhol has produced and repeated a movie-style image of him, dressed as a cowboy with a holster on his hip and a drawn gun in his hand. Warhol used screen printing to reproduce the same image over and over again.

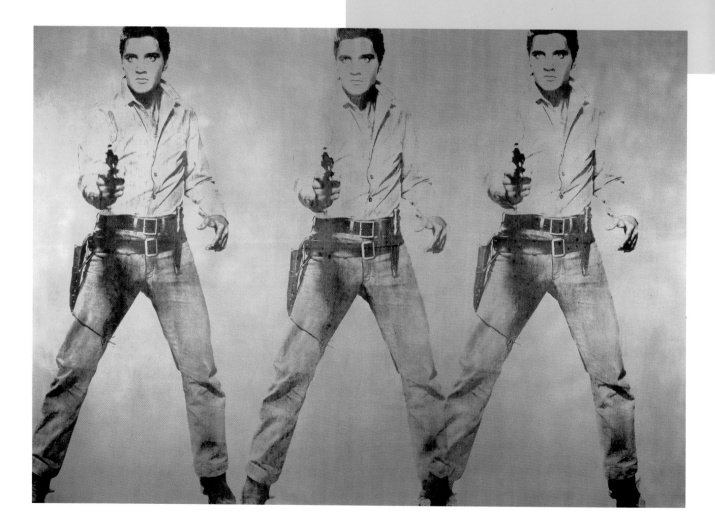

10

210 Coca-Cola Bottles

1962, silkscreen print on canvas

Like many Pop artists, Warhol made pictures of well-known products as well as famous people. This print shows the most famous soft drink of the twentieth century, Coca-Cola. Warhol has repeated the familiar bottles in rows, as if they are lined up on a supermarket shelf. He has made the picture look like an advertising poster. But, by including empty and half-filled bottles among the full ones, he shows that this is a work of art, not an advertisement.

Liz 6

1962, silkscreen print on canvas

Elizabeth Taylor, with her pale skin, jet-black hair, and violet eyes, was a very popular movie star in the 1950s and 1960s. In 1962, she starred in *Cleopatra*. Warhol made several prints of her, in a variety of color schemes. Here he has given her two arcs of turquoise eyeshadow to balance the bright red of her mouth and the background. He plays with color to attract attention – as many advertisements do.

PRINTING

The traditional way of making a print is to cut into a surface so that a design stands out on it. Then the design is inked and pressed onto a sheet of paper. This is the print. Unlike painting, the same print can usually be made again and again. Modern printing techniques include silkscreen (see page 30), which is like stenciling.

CLAES OLDENBURG (USA) born 1929

"I am for art you can sit on."

Claes Oldenburg was born in Sweden but grew up in the United States, in the city of Chicago. He worked as a journalist and then as a librarian before becoming an artist. After moving to New York, he opened a store in 1961, selling painted plaster replicas of household objects.

This led to his making giant sculptures of foods, such as ice cream, hamburgers, and French fries. For these, and for his "soft sculptures" of normally hard objects, he used various materials, from painted metal or plaster to shiny vinyl or soft fabrics stuffed with cotton or foam.

Floor Burger

1962, painted sailcloth stuffed with foam

We may see images of hamburgers advertising fast food restaurants, but we do not expect to see sculptures of them in art exhibitions. Oldenburg brought junk food to the art gallery. We would be more tempted to sit on this hamburger than to eat it. *Floor Burger* would not fit on a plate – it is more than six feet wide!

POP SCULPTURE

Most traditional sculptures are made of wood, stone, or bronze. Pop artists seldom use these. Oldenburg favors soft materials such as vinyl, leather, and canvas. Another important Pop sculptor, George Segal, makes plaster casts of real people and places them among objects such as vending machines. Segal's pale, heavy figures look somewhat ghostly and sinister.

Oldenburg likes to play with opposites. The hamburger, which we think of as fist-sized, hot, and edible, has been made here into something huge, cold, and impossible to eat.

Piccadilly Circus, London.

ET.2987R

Lipsticks in Piccadilly Circus
1966, mixed media on paper

Here we see six giant lipsticks towering over buildings, buses, and lampposts in Piccadilly Circus, an area alive with billboards, at the center of the British capital, London. To show his project for a new monument, Oldenburg cut out a lipstick advertisement from a magazine and stuck it onto a picture postcard. He has proposed several monuments of this kind. The first one actually to be built was a giant lipstick at Yale University in 1969.

Oldenburg enjoyed making food the subject of his art. These four objects look like giant ice pops. Each has a wooden stick and a bite mark cut out of one corner. They are bright and colorful, like ices, but they are made from furry animal-print fabric. Again, Oldenburg is working with opposites. He has made small, frozen, sweet-tasting ices into large, soft, strokable objects more like cushions.

Soft Fur Good Humors
1963, soft-stuffed fake fur with painted wood

13

ALLAN D'ARCANGELO (USA) born 1930

Allan D'Arcangelo was a Pop artist in the 1960s, though he later turned to abstract painting. In New York, where he worked, he was known as the poet of the American highways. His paintings were of open roads, gas stations, and traffic signs.

D'Arcangelo liked the contrast of artificial light against dark roads, trees, and skies. Most of his highway pictures are night scenes, lit by the glare of headlights and the bright glow of traffic signs and white markings.

Marilyn

1962, acrylic paint on canvas

Marilyn Monroe was the most frequently painted movie star of the 1950s and early 1960s. D'Arcangelo shows her as a cut-out paper doll, not yet fully assembled. Her face is blank, with letters by slots in place of her features. The eyes, brows, mouth, and nose have tabs marked with letters matching those on her face. The scissors hanging at the side show that the features are to be cut out and slotted into place. D'Arcangelo is perhaps saying that the star's glamorous image is not natural but manufactured.

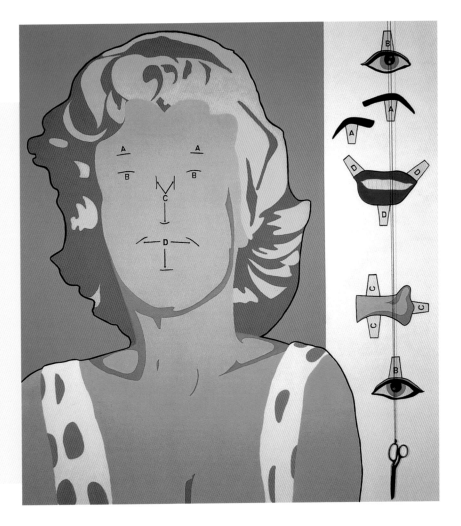

US Highway 1 – No. 5

1962, acrylic paint on canvas

D'Arcangelo made five different paintings of this straight highway. In each one we seem to have moved closer to a point on the horizon. The triangular road with its narrowing white markings makes us think that we are looking into the distance. Is there an end to this route? The highway is seen from the front seat of an automobile driving along at night. The landscape blends into the road. Far away on the right is a badge-shaped traffic sign, and on the left is the symbol of a Texaco service station. Like the nighttime driver, we see the signs out of the corners of our eyes, because we are looking at the road ahead, mentally keeping to the right of the white line.

FAME

Pop artists were fascinated by fame, and especially by stars like Marilyn Monroe, who were "made" by movies and the press. In a way, the stars were not very different from soup cans and cars. In the same way as goods were attractively packaged, stars had their appearance changed to make them appealing, That may be why D'Arcanagelo showed Monroe as a doll to be assembled, and why Warhol made repeated "production line" images.

TOM WESSELMANN (USA) born 1931

"Advertising images excite me..."

Wesselmann began drawing cartoons during his army service, and only studied art after he left. Then his collages and paintings led to his being recognized as a leading Pop artist.

He has often made pictures in series – still lifes of popular foods, or sections from modern interiors. Sometimes he stuck real or sculpted objects onto his paintings, making three-dimensional collages.

Still Life #19

1962, mixed media on board

This picture shows a loaf of sliced bread with its brand name, Rubel's American Beauty, on the packaging. Beside it is a pack of Lipton's soup mixes. A can of fruit and a bottle of ketchup both have a Del Monte label. At the back are a Schmitz Beer and a pack of Camel cigarettes. Only the apples and the cream-topped dessert are without a brand name. Brand-name products are seen as playing a central role in modern life.

Mouth #14

1967, oil paint on canvas

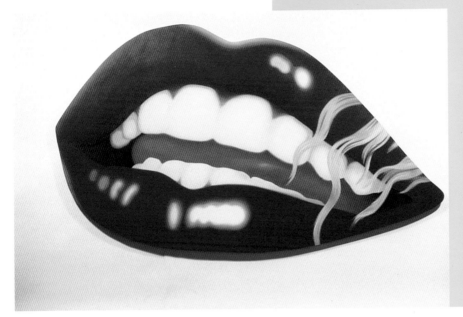

Wesselmann made a series of mouth paintings. This one looks like a picture on a billboard, seen as you ride by in a car. The perfect white teeth between shiny red lips look as though they might be advertising toothpaste or lipstick. A few strands of blonde hair have blown across the mouth, as if the person is sitting in a fast-moving sports car. But we see nothing of the rest of the face or hair – everything around the lips is cut off. A typical glamor image is isolated and suddenly seems very strange.

STILL LIFE

A still life is a picture of non-moving objects. Still-life painting has a long history, but Pop still lifes were new in focusing on brand-name products and showing them in the style of advertisements.

Interior #2

1964, acrylic and mixed media on board

Although this picture is an interior, we also see a cityscape through the window. The skyscrapers represent the changing world of the 1960s. Inside the room are several modern features of the decade. The fan, electric clock, and fluorescent light are real and working. Wesselmann has stuck them to the painted background.

JAMES ROSENQUIST (USA) born 1933

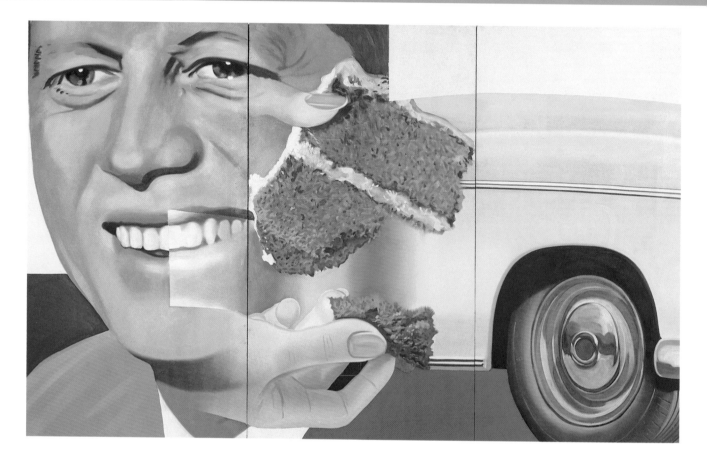

James Rosenquist first worked as a sign painter, making billboards for an advertising agency. In New York City he painted theater posters. He also created some window displays for large department stores.

In his art Rosenquist uses bright, bold images as seen on many billboards. He often takes pieces of these images and arranges them in surprising compositions. This creates a striking effect, making us look twice and see things in a different way.

President Elect

1960–61, oil paint on board

President John F. Kennedy had the good looks of a movie star and was often painted by Pop artists. Here we see a close-up of Kennedy just before he took office. Rosenquist makes a female thumb emerge from Kennedy's left eye. From his chin and neck come the finger and thumb of another hand. The hands are breaking a slice of cake. Behind this we see the wheel and part of the body of a shiny new automobile. Rosenquist puts together images from modern life in a random way. It is how we often see images in reality.

Dishes

1964, oil paint on canvas

Look at this close-up of dishes drip-drying in a plastic rack. It is something we see every day, but not something we would expect people to paint. More traditionally, artists paint still lifes showing bowls of fruit or vases of flowers. In this group of brightly colored cups, glasses, and plates, Rosenquist has added touches of bright white paint to give the effect of light glinting on the sparkling clean objects. Everything is shiny and new. It is an image from a typical 1960s kitchen.

MODERN MIXTURE

Although Rosenquist worked in the traditional, very subtle medium of oil paints, he used them like a billboard artist, creating cool, flat, bright, strongly outlined forms. His work was full of surprises because the images he brought together were unexpected and were not shown on the same scale. Compare the size of the president elect's head, opposite, with the automobile wheel.

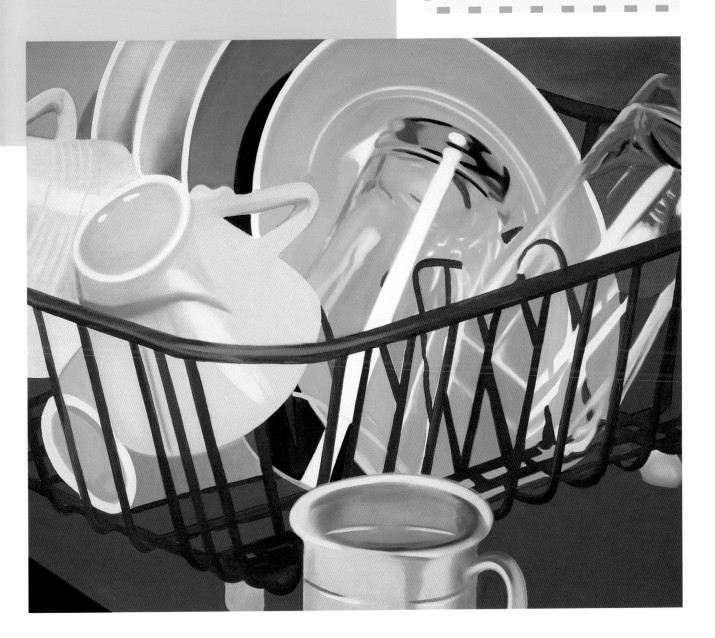

RICHARD HAMILTON (UK) born 1922

"This is tomorrow."

Richard Hamilton was one of the pioneers of Pop Art in Britain. During the 1950s he organized several important exhibitions, showing his own work and that of other artists. In 1956, his work for the famous exhibition "This is Tomorrow" introduced London to Pop Art.

Hamilton's pictures are often a mix of oil paint on canvas with other things, such as magazine photos, logos, and words. These are put together to make a collage. Hamilton has also made some sculptures. They are all images of the modern world, modern life, and modern products.

The Solomon R. Guggenheim (Spectrum)

1965–66, fiberglass and cellulose

This multicolored sculpture is a copy of the Guggenheim Museum – the modern art gallery on New York's Fifth Avenue. The building itself looks unusual because of its circular shape. Inside, visitors walk down a wide spiral ramp while they look at the paintings on the wall. The outside of the building is light gray.

In the image we see here, Hamilton has taken the shape of the museum and made it into a sculpture, about five feet tall. He brightens up the building with a rainbow effect. It looks as if colored lights are shining on the walls.

Interior II

1964, oil paint and collage on panel

MORE TECHNIQUES

Collages are cut-outs arranged and pasted down on paper or canvas. Assemblages are arrangements of objects or fragments. Some works are so hard to define that they are just called "mixed media" – a combination of materials or techniques.

Hamilton made many interior scenes by cutting up magazine images and arranging them in his own way. You can tell this is not a real room – the TV set seems to hover in space and the lamp is cut in half. Behind the chair, Hamilton has placed a picture of an actress, taken from a movie clip. She appeared in a crime movie about greed and violence. The TV screen is showing one of the most terrible events of the 1960s, the shooting of President Kennedy during a motorcade in Dallas, Texas. These images, placed in a pleasant interior, remind us of the dark side of modern life.

PETER BLAKE (UK) born 1932

Peter Blake studied at the Royal College of Art, London, where he became part of the Pop Art movement in Britain. He took his subject matter from advertisements, magazines, and comic books.

Having grown up in Britain during the difficult 1940s, Blake liked bright, modern images. He enjoyed American movies and music, and painted many stars. In 1967, he designed a famous cover for *Sergeant Pepper's Lonely Hearts Club Band*, an album by the British pop group, the Beatles.

Got a Girl

1960–61, oil paint on board with collage

At the top of this painting are six pictures of rock-and-roll musicians, all well known in the 1960s. The two pictures on the right are both of Elvis Presley, a favorite for many Pop artists. The pictures look like photos pinned to a pop fan's wall. On the left is a vinyl record with the Capitol label in its center. Capitol was a music company for which Presley and many other rock-and-roll stars recorded songs.

The Toy Shop

1962, mixed media on wood

This is a form of self-portrait, telling us about the artist's loves, interests, and activities. Blake uses a window full of toys to show us a collection of things he enjoyed in his childhood and youth. He devised the work as a way of storing many of his smallest items. Among the toys you can see badges, paints, and brushes.

By making a mixed-media display and not just a painting, Blake has recreated an old-fashioned toy shop. At first it looks like the real thing. It captures the excitement of a child looking into a room full of toys. The window frame, sill, wall, and door are child-sized. They are painted in the bright colors often used by shops to attract passers-by. *The Toy Shop* is meant to interest and amuse us, to make us appreciate objects that the artist enjoyed himself.

PATRICK CAULFIELD (UK) born 1936

Caulfield began his career in the design department of a food company, washing, brushing, and polishing chocolates for display. Later he studied at the Chelsea School of Art and the Royal College of Art in London.

Caulfield's paintings have the simplicity of some advertisements and posters. He often uses one overall color, either on its own or with just a few touches of other colors. The paint is so even that, from a distance, his pictures look like prints.

After Lunch

1975, acrylic paint on canvas

The interior of this small Swiss restaurant is entirely blue. The paler blue makes us feel that a shaft of light is shining into the room from an unseen window. A figure, in outline, is looking across at a fondue pot on the table. His bow tie and at-home attitude suggest that he is a waiter.

Inside this picture is another picture. It looks like a tourist poster of a famous lakeside castle. This is painted very accurately, like a bright color photo. Because it is different from the simplified outlines all around it, it attracts our attention. In front of the poster is a tank containing six swimming goldfish and a miniature castle. The bright orange and blue shapes stand out boldly, catching our eye.

View of the Bay
1964, oil paint on board

Here we see bright lights glinting in a dark sky and deep blue water. It is a night scene – perhaps that is why the flags look gray. The flags are bigger than anything else in the picture, so we feel as if they are right in front of us. We seem to be looking down from the balcony of a building. Everything is simplified. Only blocks of bright color are used. Boats, buildings, trees, and flags are picked out by simple black lines. The painting looks like a giant postcard.

POP COLLEGE
Pop Art was revolutionary and upset some people. But at Britain's most important teaching center, the Royal College of Art, Pop work was encouraged. Patrick Caulfield, Peter Blake, David Hockney, and other well-known Pop artists studied at the RCA.

Inside a Swiss Chalet
1969, oil paint on canvas

This painting is like a very simple print. Green is the only color – the rest is clean black line. We feel as if we are inside a wooden cabin, looking toward a room with neatly made bunk beds. We can see wooden chairs and wooden beams above wooden floors. The angle at which we glimpse the room makes us think we have just entered the cabin. The green light is calming. It gives us a cozy feeling, as if we are alone in a house, waiting for the inhabitants to return.

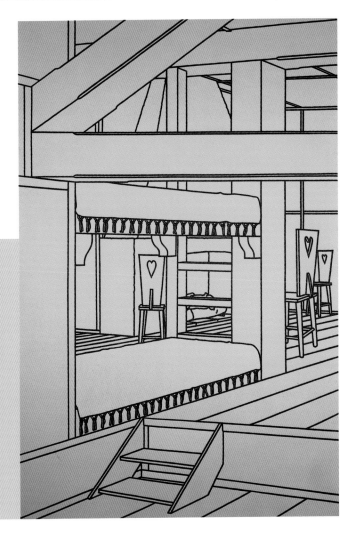

DAVID HOCKNEY   (UK) born 1937

"I paint what I like, when I like..."

Born in Bradford, in northern England, David Hockney was a brilliant student at the Royal College of Art in London. By the 1960s, he was a famous painter.

Hockney loved the hot sunshine and blue sky of California, and made his home in Los Angeles. Inspired by the lifestyle, he painted a number of bright poolside scenes.

A Bigger Splash

1967, acrylic paint on canvas

Here we see the big splash made by an unseen person who has dived from the yellow board into the pool. We seem to be at the pool's edge, looking toward the house. The weather is sunny – the sky is bright, unbroken blue. Hockney used a roller brush to paint areas such as the pool and sky, making them look flat, like an advertising poster. He made the splash effect by applying paint in different ways. First he dribbled light liquid paint over the blue to give an impression of falling water. Then he dabbed dryish white paint over it for a spray effect. Last he flicked runny white paint over the blue, to make it look like fine drops of splashing water.

Mr. and Mrs. Clark and Percy

1970–71, acrylic paint on canvas

ACRYLIC PAINTS

Hockney's most famous works of the 1960s were painted with acrylics. These are synthetic paints, made with an artificial resin, whereas traditional colors are made from natural materials. Acrylics are especially suitable for pictures with strong, flat colors, and they dry more quickly than oil paints.

This is a very large painting showing two friends of the artist at their home, with one of their two white cats. Ossie Clark and his wife, Celia Birtwell, were well-known fashion and fabric designers in the London of the late 1960s, which had by then become the style center of the western world.

The room shown here is simple, modern, and stylish. The figures have taken up non-traditional poses – Ossie is slouched in his chair, with a cigarette in his hand and his bare feet half-buried in the rug. On the wall, to the left of Celia, is a painting by Hockney, called *Meeting the Good People*. The severe lines and bareness of the room are softened by a glimpse of greenery outside.

There were many other Pop artists at work in the 1960s. Here are just a few examples of what they did. Look at their colors and images. By now you can probably pick out typical Pop Art themes.

MEL RAMOS
Man of Steel

1962, oil paint on canvas

By the 1960s Superman was widely known from comic strips, movies, and TV. Many Pop artists painted the character. Ramos (USA, born 1935) shows him bursting through a metal sheet – a true man of steel!

JOE TILSON
Transparency, the Five Senses: Taste

1968–69, silkscreen print on perspex

Joe Tilson (UK, born 1928) created a series of pictures based on the senses. This mouth represents taste. But it is half-opened, and inside we can see a starry sky, making the lips look very glamorous. The image is presented as one frame on a giant strip of film.

ED RUSCHA
Standard Station, Amarillo, Texas
1963, oil paint on canvas

Like D'Arcangelo, Ruscha (USA, born 1937) was excited by bright roadside images lighting up night skies. This gas station is made up of simple shapes and bold colors, creating a dramatic effect.

JIM DINE
Child's Blue Wall
1962, oil paint on canvas with mixed media

Dine (USA, born 1935) used a real lamp to light this painted canvas. Looking like a toy castle, the lamp makes the link with a child's room clearer.

abstract art Art that does not show images from the real world. It relies on shapes, textures, and colors to interest the viewer.

acrylic paint An industrially produced, quicker-drying alternative to oil paint.

brand name A name that identifies a particular product, so you can tell it apart from similar products made by other companies. Coca-Cola and McDonald's are well-known brand names today.

canvas A strong fabric on which artists paint.

collage A collection of materials, such as paper, fabric, and photos, stuck onto a background.

composition The way a work of art is arranged.

convenience food Food that does not need much preparation, such as canned, frozen, or dried products – even ready-made meals.

image A picture or idea.

interior The inside of a room or building.

lithography A printing method often used in modern book production, posters, and comics.

logo A design, in the form of a word or symbol, that identifies a company or product.

mass production Making large numbers of standardized products, usually using machines.

mixed media A mixture of materials, often including collage, used together in one artwork.

movement A style or period of art.

oil paint A thick paint with a buttery texture, traditionally used by many artists.

pin-up A famous person whose many fans often pin up his or her photo where they can admire it.

pioneer Someone who develops or explores something new.

popular culture The features of modern life, such as movies, television, pop music, and comics.

rock and roll A type of song and dance music with pounding rhythms, popular in the 1950s and 1960s.

self-portrait An image that an artist makes of him/herself.

silkscreen prints Images made by rolling ink over a stencil that is marked onto a taut piece of silk. The ink is forced through fine holes in the unmarked parts of the silk, onto a piece of paper or canvas.

still life An arrangement of objects that cannot move, such as fruit, flowers, or bottles.

vinyl A shiny man-made material, similar to plastic, which is often used to imitate leather.

POP TIMES

1945 World War II ends.

1947 New York becomes world art center. Major abstract art movement takes off in USA.

1951 First color TV broadcast in USA.

1956 Jackson Pollock, leading American abstract artist, dies. Richard Hamilton takes part in first Pop Art exhibition in London.

1957 First Sputnik satellite is launched by USSR (Russia).

1960 John F. Kennedy is elected President of the United States.

1961 Yuri Gagarin becomes first man in space. Berlin Wall is erected.

1962 Marilyn Monroe dies.

1963 President J. F. Kennedy is killed. First Beatles album is released.

1966 Walt Disney, world-famous cartoon creator, dies. London becomes world fashion center.

1969 Neil Armstrong becomes first man to walk on moon. Concorde makes its first flight.

1970 Beatles group splits up.

FURTHER INFORMATION

Galleries to visit

The best places to see original Pop Art works are in the United States. The **Museum of Modern Art**, New York, and the **Andy Warhol Museum**, Pittsburgh, both have excellent collections.

In Europe, the **Ludwig Museum**, Cologne (Germany) and **Stedelijk Museum**, Amsterdam (The Netherlands), also have many examples. The **Tate Gallery**, London (UK), has a number of works by various Pop artists. The **1853 Gallery**, Saltaire, West Yorkshire (UK), is a museum dedicated to the work of David Hockney.

Websites to browse

http://www.fi.muni.cz/~toms/PopArt
http://www.suu.edu/WebPages/
    MuseumGaller/Art101/popart.html
http://www.warhol.org/

Books to read

Getting to Know the World's Greatest Artists and Composers: Andy Warhol by Mike Venezia, Children's Press, 1997

Roy Lichtenstein: The Artist at Work by Lou Ann Walker, Lodestar Books, 1994

Understanding Modern Art by Monica Bohm-Duchen and Janet Cook, EDC Publications, 1992

INDEX

abstract art 30, 31
Abstract Expressionism 4, 8
acrylic paint 5, 6, 9, 15, 17, 24, 26, 27, 30
advertising 4, 6, 11, 17, 18, 22, 24, 26
automobiles 4, 15, 17, 18
Beatles, The 22, 31
billboards 7, 17, 18, 19
Blake, Peter 22–23, 25
    Got a Girl 22
    The Toy Shop 23
brand names 6, 16, 30
Britain 4, 13, 22, 23, 25
cars, see automobiles
cartoons 8, 31
Caulfield, Patrick 24–25
    After Lunch 24
    Inside a Swiss Chalet 25
    View of the Bay 25
cities 13, 17
Coca-Cola 11, 30
collage 6, 13, 16, 20, 21, 22, 30
colors 5, 6, 7, 8, 9, 11, 19, 20, 23, 24, 25, 26, 27
comics 4–5, 8, 9, 22, 30
convenience foods 6, 16, 30
D'Arcangelo, Allan 14–15
    Marilyn 15
    US Highway 1 – No. 5 14–15
Dine, Jim 29
    Child's Blue Wall 29
Disney, Walt 31
exhibitions 10, 20, 31
fabric 12, 13
Guggenheim Museum 20
Hamilton, Richard 20–21, 31
    Interior II 21
    The Solomon R. Guggenheim 20

highways 14, 15
Hockney, David 25, 26–27
    A Bigger Splash 26
    Mr. and Mrs. Clark and Percy 27
Indiana, Robert 7
    The American Dream I 7
interiors 16, 17, 21, 24, 25, 27, 30
Kennedy, President J. F. 18, 21, 31
Lichtenstein, Roy 5, 8–9
    Drowning Girl 9
    Mr. Bellamy 8
    Sunrise 9
    Whaam! 4–5
light 7, 14, 19, 20, 24, 25, 29
lithography 9, 30
logos 6, 20, 30
London (UK) 13, 22, 27
machines 5, 7, 10, 30
magazines 4, 6, 20, 21, 22
mass production 6, 10, 30
mixed media 13, 16, 17, 21, 23, 29, 30
Monroe, Marilyn 7, 15, 31
moon 31
movies 4, 10, 21, 22, 28, 30
movie stars 7, 10, 11, 15, 18
oil paint 6, 7, 8, 9, 11, 17, 18, 19, 20, 21, 22, 25, 27, 28, 29, 30
Oldenburg, Claes 5, 12–13
    Floor Burger 12
    Leaning Fork with Meatball and Spaghetti I 5
    Lipsticks in Piccadilly Circus 13
    Soft Fur Good Humors 13
outline 5, 8, 9, 24, 25
paintings 4, 7, 8, 9, 14, 15, 16, 17, 18, 19, 21, 22, 24, 25, 26, 27, 28, 29
photos 20, 22, 24, 30

pin-ups 10, 30
pop music 10, 22, 30
popular culture 30
posters 6, 7, 9, 18, 24, 26
Presley, Elvis 10, 22
prints, printing 5, 6, 7, 9, 10, 11, 24
Ramos, Mel 28
    Man of Steel 28
rock and roll 10, 22, 30
Rosenquist, James 18–19
    Dishes 19
    President Elect 18
Ruscha, Ed 29
    Standard Station, Amarillo, Texas 29
satellite 31
sculptures 5, 12, 13, 20
Segal, George 12
self-portraits 23, 30
silkscreen printing 6, 7, 10, 11, 28
skyscrapers 17
still lifes 16, 17, 19, 30
Taylor, Elizabeth 11
television 4, 8, 21, 30
Tilson, Joe 28
    Transparency, the Five Senses: Taste 28
traffic signs 14, 15
vinyl 6, 12, 22, 30
Warhol, Andy 6, 7, 10–11, 15
    210 Coca-Cola Bottles 11
    Four Colored Campbell's Soup Can 6
    Liz 6 11
    Marilyn Diptych 7
    Triple Elvis 10
Wesselmann, Tom 16–17
    Interior # 2 17
    Mouth # 14 17
    Still Life # 19 16
World War II 4, 11, 23, 31